Designated Heartbeat

BRUCE ANDREWS

SALT

CAMBRIDGE

PUBLISHED BY SALT PUBLISHING

PO Box 937, Great Wilbraham, Cambridge PDO CB1 5JX United Kingdom

First published 2006

Printed and bound in the United Kingdom by Lightning Source

Typeset in Swift 9.5 / 13

ISBN-13 978 1 8447 068 3 paperback
ISBN-10 1 84471 068 8 paperback

SP

1 3 5 7 9 8 6 4 2

Contents

Acknowledgments

Thanks to the editors and publishers for earlier presentations of these pieces: *American Letters & Commentary, And, Angelaki, Atelier, Avec, Big Allis, Capilano Review, Chloroform, Denver Quarterly, Hot Bird Mfg, I Am A Child: Poetry After Bruce Andrews & Robert Duncan, Mandorla, O.ARS, Outlet, Pig Cupid, Poettext, Primary Writing, Shiny, Stet, Sic & Sp., Verse, Zing.*

I Knew the Signs by Their Tents

Obligation for hire
lexicon seduces
personally notwithstanding
add?
consummate alarm—
ulterior? Stain
fling incarceration by rumor
punctual beauty pink
dissembling punctual crawlers only later
said meaning was riding her
covert inside capsuled
rumor sweets can compare
forgive slip
withhold stunned show twice commensurate
consummate frigid perceiveless
italic hesitation
that rosy 'System' is an owner
atmosphere breaks—ransoms—heart
little white dot
name
sharp
alibi
orbit
bubble nothing is
amiss price kiss implied
stop on spot
peculiar eye tint
nor any menace
logic
fundamental signals
dream not broken it
absorb terse sums—
Basis—teeth balked

unforeseen intimate
scene a thing
urgent gown
rub esoteric shame jealous
root is freely certified
on view breeds to ratify
bother and betrayed fit *at hand—*
delicious negotiation collapsing feast
I'm all suspended
about the outside of myself
surroundings inscrutable temperature expositor
nothing proves the news
experience consumes on plan
hip incidents
could this be you
could this be you
could this be you
delusive fickle
to be denied, never let me go
unimpeachably disco
spigot job, o.k.
cuddle can punish prism =
svelte disheveled affront
realms to compromise's Ground Floor
aggrandized prompter coming in
contrite passive prompter legs
out of a dream world licensed souvenir
flesh tilts away
suit me up to familiarities
tumult elite
edifice remote
parsing is the manufacture vain
would nice to falsify buccaneers

go to unobtained trouble enhances
enables a guy with superstitious value
text structure so yawn
que viva secrets unsubstantial find it innocent
license for proof
& trappings the worthless function
yes, rhetoric withdraws to be so sad
hem is fair
cease in retrospect
but a little, we know
nominate *these* cliff-hangers
arithmetic of negligence
enclose the neck in charms
syllable economy
where functions depose
cut me in for a loss
can any magistrate *afford*
to *recognize* mock *heroics?*
Hairbreadth's crescent
tentacles the case
chastened suck to paragraphs prompt & straight
the apparatus of loss
together pattern conquested hands redress
sweet incarnation premature instead
infinite suspect size dress only me
trust adjourns
convertible ordinary honey am dumb
in process show me this and this
inner forfeit exhaled distinction
law tint
bliss with a Delete—threat's
presence had cool schemes
sueted up their own gender

it must be no width concern
repetition didn't subscribe
fact foreclosed unsuspecting female
orthography unburdening the drawers
invalidates nobody
slit we perfected sign surrounded tight excuse
strategy entertains
the limits—fond as fallible
inform your signifying about your nails, sugar
plush limitations curtseying intercourse
off-limits with incendiary requisite
glowing corners
progressively hear figures depositing
alarm to dazzle coming negatively homestead so near
perpetual occasion for castration
straighter to be carried up
in lids suffer error now
fear of moments the error
barometer hers the sumptuous
in prime mechanics of sleaze
outside enchanted ground
intimate creature
circumstance statement fairies
adulterous adulatory bees
another hour on me
lips without surprise
cervically audacious satin
mercy's library semen
aim of Irony prefix at discount
seam became wick ourselves
adjoining loaded heat
body drips censure
a practice

doubt
throat
ecstatic curls
and forget help
to keep baffle
corkless throat have tried
low erect
clue awful
ring tightens blunder to regulate
cocoon tease version of sweeps
artisanal difference admission
incubates income acquaintance
wet trouble
body warranted possibility through scant pricklier
labor—privilege's interdict
null heart marketeers esteemed
censure
small whim capsized
subjugated toast
circumference aghast

Verbal Sallies

June	15–16	88
June	16–17	88
June	17–18	88
June	19	88
June	20	88
June	22	88
June	23–24	88
June	26	88
June	27	88
June	28	88

dear Sally—

love,

Bruce

1.

100° honey hush—diddent!—the sweat
melts telegraph-boy hats lips barely
close hoops to decide
rallentandos swept loose.
Nobody seems to be breathing lickage
libre
periphery & even beyond blur cyclic *soirées.*
Lilliputian skinny-dip atom
poised in parallel material privacy
draw an imaginary bow grilles around
it fool's gold elevations.

2.

Skidding, ready, hone—
dearer—
spin—
bouts light can carve
one more species
fervor cordage.
Classics repent: I can't
afford the tradition
shouldn't wrap up
I swear—pretends—predict
lucks tucked underneath the much
unforgettable flickers—referent burn-out
stitched leisure headshots of standbys, dram
lines
looks arraign
emotion on the skin.

3.

In mid-
leap phasized
singled in vascular clockwork amplify
by wiring against a black drop
shows you arms. Cross-
word—maps decolonized—the entwining
intermittences—in rhythm—
upside
hope scuttles
that massing susceptibility or be
stopped short
vie yessum but bites
treadle stroboscopic
there's your stemwinder, animal elastic
ventilating kiss could remind.

4.

Happy dictation. Stage-
struck—as if—
mammal less
brief bluish glue
lightening
nape fwd insigniac
vicarious fact box.
Delusions of reproof recognizably dizzy
at a faster or slower
things vertigo
intervening
query as can be.
Oh, I win the pool!
Lank
taper
baste
necklike pecking disorder—
apertures mollified
ornaments precipitately.

5.

If you stop standing on your head
slices of pink rubbery sap
plumed orchids backward
= indirect answer. Fold comma
number milk revamps
given care zeal—
metaphoric outdoors feint, yeah.
Ultra ecto
via rewires rescind
lip ruffle floppy desk, torso blur
anticipatory piranhas. Mute
is king
satin pre-op
hex
giveth red.

6.

Click
solve it captive
silked claque away—
act the public,
my thinking can sensate
for itself. Stethoscopic
nova questionnaires,
marzipanic seersucker
made by bloom en-
genderable
smudge list—do
tell! Apostrophe
bubble—turns page—
unfence pinwheel casing
open-air relents.
Movies mahogany
by tugs pretty polly
suspend between
ombudsperson
lips that
barnstorm fix.

7.

Bravo playfully
furor *de luxe*
curvature velocity
faster at night. Arc
trespass petal
indistincture
unbreakage by intent to
as does emphatic grouping
cellularly shake
the rattles withholding blanks.
Pendulum
calliope practical lighting—
composite enables hex
static hatch
helm volumetric—peripheral sparks,
distinct buzzes
fine as frogs' hair
most pointedly delighted.

8.

Listening for portraiture
sweep the jokes overword
ticktock palette disown
least wire mute supply.
Pup-pet pup-pet. But what will happen?
Treat a trick
can take it—
strobe fix color scheme color fault—
ruckus ineffortably
restack canonic multiplication nerves
guess acoustic o'clock. Monotone
wands lime babalu
stress short—
frantic slow motion.

9.

Aah—
bay (okay)
hah (true)
hum (noise)
ma (no)
men (make)
say (ants)
ten (to me)—
auto-da-fé curtain-bow to
this is less time
cake-frosting white pinball
scan to form pages
and absolutely anomalous large as birds' eggs—
a loan word—
shed light
beeswax
unclenching too appliqué *tropico*
 hedonic eccentric caches.

10.

Lace
pyrite triggering bellwether
hand resting on the opposite shoulder
will yet be read
no more than visual caress all
primates except man vertigo discount—
mid-pointed co-signs dressed up to the eyes
lucky and unlucky dovetailing
mix same proof—
blind by short'nin'
not the incidental scenery. Night
begins with history.

"Facts are Stupid Things"

Heart's tackle pulse
shears shapeless
                    digest   enflamed voluntaries
          whet on tumble force from here
    to already here cuts off
                              circumstances, less inside
              come off it insist which
                        clone is original night
                        eyelets steepling the cheeks.
              Synchonativity
                    servo-machinists
    melody—
    feedback with good manners
                              contempt
breeds repetition.   Buffer books boot
              blush volley body levied
          copy mouth's
                        kindle at suggest what retracts is due.
              Pencil up wrongs
                    a little filler on the whole
                          top full foaled
                anatomy venom to pardon part
                by teeth spider in a spoon,
          pygmy gum chastising
                    underprop too clean for edges.
    The yielded set—hold that lapse!
    Hum span the contrivance
    tilts, bulldozes
                          change the unacquainted
                lips counterfeit module bias
                gives head to cull
                froth ribs = malice.   Pluto
                        relented vaunt

                                    doll blot bated
                        befits seeming assonance & hardness
                                    administer hips
                    in serving plates extend
                    to palm the skim escort layers.
            Repair interrupts, keeps habits
from disinterested overrefinementals — practice your peaches.
            Smack or no motion
            impulse resolution clutters on the spot, titles
                from coops requital
                pledged in with expedient to pause — sorry,
                mink; have is have unthread
                the eye, the deserved of all observed;
                a page of clouts
                                too respective in undeterred differences.
                                    Seizure do your scrub
                                    this morning out of the day
                                    half-blown to adulterate
                    autocracy's body conjointly bed your deeds —
                                soft petitions
                        mousing the shorts
                                    off multi-tempered
                        minute of truth rank in spate,
                    & decision creates
                                    allowance underwrought
                & overmined. Issue vibrate
                                    mess & cathechize
pineal blots
                            innocence smells consent-like
                            even almost
                assurance betrothed
                        eat anonymous part poison
                        accoutrement to cull

        [18]

the perves of best unblotting.
Secret clip conceit
understands immediate leisure
to outface fragment quantity
                                        gauze toys
            scope instance unvex
                                aphid mark sociably
                                sinewed sign
                                farms the word
                                    squeak on banquet.
            Teach us some rude.
Lineal
scathe rated
wax, forerunner
of cavity spurns restraint
for compulsion
                        coil covet
bitters bright sheath publishing
to this hand to souse
                    & swoop.   Dishabit
                    backslid genealogy
        safe to reverse beckon pre-op
    floor pays for knuckles
                        endommagement
                        plotted sashay
                        haste occasion stuns
                        the will, diapers the pill open to urge
        a certain amount of tangling up
        into things pin broke
                        sex hush con-
    verts discarded puns to brief the womb.
                    Fake precedent, recharge shocks.
            Flatter soothes up incite

to suggest tame
to task thick-ribbed
goosebumps appetited tooth.   Gap
galls, gall gaps
Check the whirl warrant
stains usurping down
cheeks clear to pour
speed in the flattering
tablet the brief
rights & the abstract compels.
Closer jacket.   Brace made tense—
unyoke's pencil guilt
shared the manage of my heart sponges
your medicine of my economy
to speed out sparks.

Did You Really?

I sulk a good line. Lickish damp sympathetically helmful special insular thrown views, defibrillating sundown in a notary public kind of way. Horizontal spottings stir the mute by reciprocity. Still when by yourself only an instant can make a memory.

Facts deeds on hook do join vamp at the same orthographic sentiment. To house the apartment with kissing authority uses dinettes too. Let's too trashy sheath claws intact lacing legs tinied the call, cool neck by pitons; implicit fan info humid elongate seduction chiding jaguar in its lethargy, stigma can get up with its hennish asterisks.

A blister where? A knob in our facts at the horizon, smoke from empire-burning forgotten brands of vulnerable philosophically generous scoopings of peeping tops & toms he's registering with ulterior suck on yells. If we notice your eyelids, are you supposed to notice ours? Repining calculates when is slang a verb & why; we had faith but as an exception. Cursory slobbering. Subscribe to?

Without gears, *no bunching.* Let's see what apes do & then see how impressed we are

The law of comparative advantage took pills. Rampant edges sides corners ribs & indentations, jarred, cadred aftermath coltish sardonic touchstone—I could go on & on—didn't it get funded?— semantic hayride the flatness, or ganglia repels the grown-fast utterances, lethargic condoms, mandible citizenship fastened on a vastness as fault.

Tends to tract tram over cerebrate pout for adrift underwater aggravation [the hems show] seize repossible Ripon society of inflammables. What sticks is content in curlers nautical by tempo. Servient self-roadblocked, foresight's capitulation—soldier wakes up in battle: promptbook, for fear. Accident insomniac, I was *on purposing* for you finally call it the elusive contagion—how many phone-calls?

Inculpatory digital ego nudge a verdict. Trimmings, couple hours at best, zealish rushless custard by the numbers, gels set free, don't give up, slow down. Fables of non-resistance stems, at once. What could lips periodicity this drastic unmeltable explosive delicacy? Recidivision—the burn marks are its flowers.

Utopia starts flat. Remember to forget the forgetting to remember. Where we inter-says depictomatic in invisible ink, vast singles go forward. Nothing squeezes the guardians of fastness, thoughts gone sappy in brigade-formation levelling of evidence our wishful thinking is editing. Vice verse exit virtue visa—splice of time— double or twice? Faction the more all of. Nemesistic stageset prince, framed & sentenced, game verb!

Searchlight practice-test: I could project into exasperate the cartoon lustongs (sic) count me twice pinking futures. Can't help the commas.

Hushing this word over cliff prevents tell me pointing now: no images of inland water—(where do they make the rivers?)—blame bed hips anchor reluctance to redundancy. Equivalent toting by a command in its legroom, underwater peril regs overdigested.

Enough excitement diagonally [deter]. Form may shun the archaic as awesome pre-yupped malls deputize those regrets. I could grow up!—hystortion everything thing poking clarity on a binge, easy does it, trappings abrupt clutch heed scarred pillow. You gets the apartment to listen. You've been bookworming early, V-effect the homeless, I can't hear our glued self summery pre-op. Some other time.

The late symbolists do wonder about memory, the protective coloring really sticks out of the box. Secret goners, dating maze's petting zoology. Describe prescribes a mattress is thought at wrong speed barbecues any exteriorize you'd wager, burying the novelistic. Offgoing & on lettage defensive is arresting divanishment to seek abdication.

Use both hands on the face. The reading could take lots—ruining a shrug on a prairie saturnalianally tightened—puny notch, the corners cut me. *But sentences can't unfold the face.* Sound of loose change fall down in the other room, the curbs are pretty flush.

You pull while I rake, you bellied up in an addendum. Attenuating a safe mirage got lost in unawaited trappist touches & sexed fruit hidden from inequality-clogged goof. Division could be a hobby, the mere fact that you're sociably something risk by the numbers.

Creamside dynamite as prosthetic rayon by diplomacy. You're pretty out. [Still fencing?] [cf.] nap applause—can a thousand plateaus be far behind? A cactus on your thinking barricaded by ghosts victimized by skin jellies hesitate near alarm. Which fossil will cut it?

Electricity breakage & that's no lie, majoritarian clairvoyance, paranoia's allegory—beers, start-up selective jot out, ramp bevies, drop your bows, or bows, take your drink, take your drink, what was your opening line? If I mention X in a vat [pone] *the gloves come off:* lofty scenic news, salve two, owning up to toss worrisome fandom. The definitive pre-inventoried chill out diaspora. Withheld is not forget, steam by mention.

[23]

You're spouting a veto, homing pigeon on left side two to tango. As if it were natural to sit down.

The modifiers formed a union, a wad has unfeeling pension punch can count so baste the version for virtue. Pernot bindery.

The robber shifts from loud cursing belligerence upon apprehension to. . . .

The channel can fit you in the joints the slots deserve less stress, kinetoscope on the skids squid with purses slugged myself radial you. Rank these groups for smell. Boast in the chest conjures the nets prawns can nominate, signage max gang the fizzles quizzical dirigible lust.

The escabeche of night rust at leisure. Bluish temporaries darkness stands to wait heat refuses alphabet batten on somnambulism.

Stress in a skirt zorro derrick under the skirt. Curricular fiancé.

GOING / INTO / RESPECT / DEPTH—little 'x's. Pantomime your waist spawning is as yoked up erect deflates inside rubber or inside skin. Incandescent lap do I have a lap too?

La libertad 're-up' in stationery rapacious as beak wand, the cocoon gets calls by agenda incubation. 'Proposition'—propositional preposition imp on leash talkage winner's hermeneut circle aromata, sizzly deadend keep from pleating.

Even a sex-change would mean jewelry tray at vacuum squatter reality; glyphic atmo-. Kleptophobia synesthesia or synthetic anaesthesia entrapment by dawn porridged devices: wet your chisel, fetish'd agronomy.

I swell at the word toppings *sucred* daun't, tenses on your side, mica enough for all. Flamenco seems to me, satisficing by alignment meant nerve verved plaque this hearting I've tendencied, no squelch by habit, no disappointment without proportional representation.

Every skill as dutyfree relate free-for-all [dative] to buy-the-hour [strokabation]. Patch up buntless, sackage. Trade creameried sequin jockies resigning the letter didactation. Reminions the. Less stern stem what . . . connects . . . anywhere strop point hunger somebody . . . caliphs &, the query bent over gladly. Journeyish, the gyros are goosing radar, the vehicle came equipped. Don't raise your chin at me—lower lips.

Lives in Bed in Hallway

Outmoving the, outfrequenting the—   Flippers now colloidal.
Can't float in the logic, exhausted escape habits, choked swim-
ming as a phrase. Dapper delegates? Withheld worth's cowardice,
shiver by name. I can't need form. Geometry farms. Inside is
Close. Vectors from inside out delirium yesterday. Terse ask.
Specialists disappear, techno-mono. Slang up, yeah? Quiet is a
critique. Fond as blasts. Craze with nothing not knowing. The
blasts are coming off dice on your head. A kind bends around
leaving. Two two. Mobile flavor units easing into eternity. Canopy
hegemony, pardon the creatures ending. Girls, is this lapidary?
Triple vapid, the harmonic misfires are forming a Union. Goose
the substance pronto. *Charm all vertical.* Loving this colorless,
metallically dangerous breathe to mark statutory instigations.
A flake in vacation. Synapse has its own luggage. Slapping pinks
slatting hands. Kneels of boss tongue. Latex motion to be aloof.
Custody got late-tags indelibly custarded. Hoops zined. A suspi-
cious voluntary. Templated heart ovum. Sulk schottische. Self
volunteers for paradigms. Infallible sobs. Silence jilted. Nothing
gathers the walls around you. Silver is knickknacked to death.
Strength of your shun. Edges this ragged. Geometry it's gone.
The blood's favorite game show. Equofinality.

Somehow That's Just The Way It Is And I Just Don't Really Care

Not a sign of people—My brains are in my heart—Why is my
heart so frail?—To be circumspect—Life's machinery—And far
more alarming—It's permissible—To your size—The bad in every
man—Keener reception—Do you mean—Nature is hard to deny—
No one belongs to me—Why behave?—I behave—No ambition—
No desire—And that's why some are nervous—Unphotographable
—In toto—I could have bound you too—Estrange me—And that-a
is that-a—Verbatim—It's only natural—Too much—I'm your slave,
dear—Conceal it—Is part of the scheme—Fools rush in—Taking
things apart now—To be—Now I believe—Matter over mind—Of
opposite sexes—And read every line—With the well-known
double-cross—You have what I lack myself—To go your own sweet
way—What's the use of trying not to fall—My possession—The
sun won't set on our possessions—Convention I break—
Horizontally speaking—It was all prearranged—You forget your
alphabet—Change your wishes to demands—That I'd be playing
solitaire—But should she refuse to succumb—*Hush, hush; quiet*—
By four hands—Troubles will keep—I can't win but here I am—
Together

Secret Refracted Somewhere Here

sentiment fallout toy

deeds halfpulled

lasso sights

pamper curb such   reap up at all

invisibly belate suddenly

if—wish, weren't

secrets, sleepwalk shirk

unwrappered over thought pageantry

tonsil doctor

splat your piece

snuggling pretext

bustibles severe

western roll at your age

inside shortsleeve

preside perfectibly what for

slice nearby one of our

defiances, what ain't

miniaturize each monad

reassuring bodyparts

success sewage

can't doting most sudden

fixed fool to be seam

attentive badge direct

pearl-like latent

turns gain why with you

look t my violence before

would we're, but seismic blame

the burst conditional

bossed over jasmine

how it bleats

gossip dementia

                                        your out amiability
                            narrow borrow ex-
                                turrets in arms
                abrupt is sore more dosed than
                    had siege a light where deed's piebald
                underhand islands or abridge tears
                            whispering laced planetary instance
                                ventilate actuarials
            ladle first
                        riviera in foreskin
                                            differently as if
                elsewhere starts, so either   by your shouldn't
                    edit waiting, move meant possible
        studded to itself
                                            deminimaleyes
                                        widen combats voice
                    to scare up
                                                translate bastards
                            framed sin sign
                                            plush option

        deflect at buy 's deal
                                maybe while preposterous
                                    the norm luck, against always
                    integer what if didn't didn't
                    forget which abetted
                                                    seduce pores
                            pressure splash dilate
        fuckup farewell
                            in & of gown
                    disappear your scopes
                        about to top

                              rapid in panning stilts
                                guarantee affect
                    open depicts please
                    goosed
                        miracle foresight

        off in as when, disarray you
      more suddenly
            latent so not incessant
            I debit the category
                              retentions all you
      why you yet doubles join you but
            elongate excludin' enunciate honey
                                    whatever had, could
                                    if the tame bunch

        this with as tacit into up
            but is tell me talk the same
      bent in cuz kept debridely

mispaginate
            a cream of verbal meaning
                              figmenting force the hectical way
                              we width

Countless

syllable talking stop possessive
to buzz
pores, unproud, slow into
question up the rafters, particular
any time surprise, you mean
at best organic
enclosure act slightest, delight space
I'm a declension even betting
thumb about, coward
queue to motif
it, maybe clocks back laminate
story, morale, douse
in turn pens off so
blotchier, face in
comma your, is it *shall* or *will*
zigzag, haven
to nominate everyday
caulk deed responsibly
sudden, we soon, dots yonder
out of yet, blurs, nutrient
opportune to sponge bask
care, *caliente*, laughs
less chapped reasons
for reasons, rejoinder
indexically daft

Count

not like, except
for, arraign attend
though, or by half
tricky, so you, enough
often where, or had,
foist, any spill, met
direct, this direct
fabric loads
dice a lock on teeming
easy blind
hands, in shout
on their own, members peel
even if far back talk at
when, abdomenizer already
contrite this much than fooling
this moist, some tease with
unable regret, am not
happenstance, you did stairs
least at the least can
sidle, pretty casual of that
off a metronome, I mean less flat
about it than that
home soon, told
or mineral, second reprieve to forget

Spinto

Total sign operator, momentary
meat device, surreptitular bend
the sappy moment—levity multiplication simulant
gut up excess metaphor—barbaric leverage enlargement:
cancel self, a global spree compendium, tentacle huckster
sense arbitrary
arbitrary imposter
evidence most cheap prayer
denudes ingenuity closure
suggestively sibilant; dense grid intervenes—
cessation function insinuate artifice
animation felicity minutiae-izing
transitive effects versus osterizer memory
undercertified on par dismounter of language
divest distance separates custodial
self-pollinating assassin—pincers
write everything as miniaturized innocence, scopo-narcotic
meticulousness *in* engorgement
to alienate umbilical equilibrium—scope scatters public
swarm
bruise
mass
precarious aperture incites
to self-concede
everyday life owns the morphology

Time Expansion

```
        1
A   h           Y   a           S   i   g   n

        2
c   u   m   u   l   a   t   i   v   e   l   y
g   o   o   e   y

        3
t   h   e           h   a   —   h   a   —   h a
i   s       s   k   i   t   t   i   s h

        4
w   i   t   h           h   a   l   o   g   e   n
l   i   p   s

        5
m   a   t   i   n   e   e
d   o   u   b   l   e           —       y   o   u

        6
t   h   e   n           m   u   r   d   e   r
a           m   o   n   a   d

        7
t   h   e           c   r   u   d   e
i   s           f   a   b   u   l   o   u s

        8
s   t   i   n   g
p   l   e   a   t   s
s   t   a   g   e
```

```
      9
n     o     t           s     o
s     t     u     t     t     e     r


      10
O     V     E     R     F     L     O     W     S


      11
p     e     a     k
n     e     c     k
n     e     s     t


      12
a     m     b     u     s     h           t     h     e
f     u     c     k


      13
a           p     r     o     n     o     u     n
w     i     t     h           a
l     e     a     s     h


      14
s     t     i     l     l
t     h     u     m     p     i     n     g
a     f     t     e     r


      15
n     e     o     l     o     g     i     s     m
o     r           t     y     p     o     ?
```

16
i n d e l i b l e
l i c k s , m a j o -
r i t a r i a n
k i s s e s

17
b e c a u s e i s
d e c l i n e

18
s t a r s b u c k l e
u p

19
C o n n i p t i o n a l -
l y Y o u r s ,

20
a d r e a m i s a
m o u t h i n
e q u i v a l e n c e

Black

white adhocism
white adolescent
white attribution
white bed
white claimant
white disruptions
white era
white fungible
white giveaways
white hour
white I
white jerk
white kelvinator
white less
white matter
white no
white out
white prearrangement
white quiescence
white rap
white stupidity
white *tipico*
white [unintelligible]
white vote
white who
white xerox
white yanking
white zeitgeist

Devo Habit

Hucksters bundle up detachment hives grows uselessness comfy to politicize a retina. The gauge of illusion as illusion: experience is life—that is, therapy fuels longshot plantation. Only absence of telos self-satisfaction's superfluity chinks. Bits outrage neo directness as brain condom. Insist = privilege = art control. Hysteria lack just repression secrets relaxed futurity, dwelling arrogant claims attachment's lack of words writing without worms. Antientropic ghost status, nonbeguiling orgy to object status ideas ready for things, readier than things. No ideas but in sexism; only coldness is frank. Idiotic team-up non-humans to fear non-death complacency makes robot repair unnecessary. Limits severely frigid grid tempo talent pre-exacting. Function needs a fiction: it belies hope by not being resisted enough. To err is statemental. Suggestion just talk & sincerity fabrication imitation. Vital signs terminate words, the lonely gone past barriers to manage gnosis trouble form better than life permission ego hang-up. Strength gives up hatchet job for the finite coaching the exact. A suspicious religious suburb copy feeling up a goose-step careened anything life belief more than system's studious rigidity to cause a harbor of belief system effects. Handicappers as cause-and-effect landscape never really happens to prefer more anthemic ads. Follow the animals as *they* roam for food too, purely happens as drug doctrine little thoughts not a sense of humor to resume normal intrusion procedure.

BIEBER LINE

Tiffany puncture service. Bouffant wetlands, gigglers on the left:
'oh, nothing'. Slur touts vita headlock, to irrigate the useful
content-haunted dial-a-fib. Sieve in a showdown. Hard rock guam
= bachelor lizard but vows barbecue the jury. Says zsa zsa. I
stabbed my hand because it was gay. Posse peers heartache
liquidators, stoolie smash-up egghead autobody ratio flaps. Use
your lips as a hamper. Here's a sentence worth reading out loud.
Fools per cake, linch-pin pop-up parade coagulant. White big.
Chemical sortège stitches on the blessing = lift this to spawn
beanie send-off, my little fact. Your job flaps are showing.
Sanitized bulking hammer pulp. Let me spigot the retro sobriety
pre-buys = death by lottery, sugar deposition ortho-goggles.
Victory slush rosy unseizureable bob, torrid or tame price crux
culinary bedding floodlights make you smell. I keep forgetting
the glowing indifference to heroin masks implicit masculinist
bias. Tie your net worth to a bungee cord. Mini-duty tweak its
belief in feline subpoena welcome center heaters never win.
Rectal brandname, stunts happen to you. Colonized patio hope
clams up fanatic slack; surrogates want praxis too, networking
the pixies. Tail wags voyeur, effortlessly bosomed. Fix me up with
a rat race. Cut the crush cranking the carefree mattress for
munchkins, demo = bloodhound the center cannot bleed. Quality
kitsch, overendowable slime. Use your scab for a bookmark.
Touch gala diagnostic curtsy—testosteronally statemental
thesaurus gets brighter marketing the slur. Call *me* cash?
Cheaters rise toward cream? Honk if you love dichotomies: FEAR
THE POLICE—juxta-poised insistence on persistence, a juried
cumshot. Spurn the rim clump that wish rigor victor temp skim
off angles. When you retire you become ammunition. Skylit
stymie muffle cling, nightie with chin-straps. Drink yourself into

a discount. Deceased by owning deep shit holograms too many
care violations—consider this a formal thump.

Lasting Kiss Removal

[for Lewis Klahr's
Tales of the Forgotten Future (Parts 1–4)]

Is your language podium-fresh?

My skeleton is comfortable

Headless

Rib cage wobble power in

R O A R Y   R U M B L E R   S P A Z

Meat blankets atilt in a hive —

> Robot sauce
>
> Aerial testes

[C A P S or no: *can't decide*]

Bounce the slice.
Scatter cursive curette magnum

Depot buzz's — on the map is ~~almost juxtapose~~

Almost juxtapose hotrod subside —

Modernism means *short*.

A L L
D E S I R E
I S
I N V E N T O R Y.

Foreground blur-flowerable keyhole

Crooner insect nosegay scam

Crucifix *toilette* opportune—

        Cub scout layaway.

        Powwow puritan hits sperm new high.

        Let X be flash, reverence head.

        If the brain did ploughing.

        Butterfly net made of voyeurist meat.

A jittery half life clef quit elusive chamois sordid

Torts a haircut chink in the pigment melody

Maybelline blindfold cupcake pantyslant

In squall frame decapitalized, tuftlike not

Pull-out manicure haptic a vaseline forager—

        Penis in frightwig, *inside* the *inside*.

Hypo

Telstar

Fond—sac, exploitation

Forcefield waits for you to condense mannerisms:

H   I   F   I

Daredevil dinosaur snakebites repressed above synch-sound

Excavate rave buzzer armrest fellatio dating sputnik

Pep flukes bodyish

Edsel cola stationwagon porn decoding

Plasma in that layered look—

remptive

ulb

Stencil eggs root in lips-foreshortened strobe—

Certainty chevronhead.

Ectosplasmic call-waiting.

Medicinal sin, insurrect vomit.

Geisha sentence sells.

Decoy duty

ALL SHOCK FRAUD

Vacuum up a hundred wind-up marbles.

Your asshole = the Bermuda Triangle.

J.F.K. in dive—Wetter no scoop winner I go smear

Syncopate over code assassins—

Cartoon Jesus.

Fur-wrapped last call.

White daub utility swirl on ice:

Loom huge, labor-intensive oven?

Girls cheat on desks.

Blockading nighttime.

U T H B U C

foam   fight

Letter-sweater zipper tick, *b y e*, clench micro stature flare

For whom the plate rises

Exhilarate lipstick substitutes poly-society

Tipsy redden fibber flag, encrustation focus

        Mood op goggle teasing =

        Tomorrow is a two-way street.

Trophy touch bossa-handed piechart velocity

Saran brood pasteurize forehead provisioning

Slink chirp Che noir bodytype mastodon attracts—

        Nozzle deny home megaphone iris.

        Surveillant numerical gridding caprice.

Little shocks neck groom chocolate-titled

Gang ass the dream graduates

Tinsel enema gyp gauge

Jungle plural frontal halo—

        KINKS R US—medicinally leveraged.

Neckishly—Buttock handsaw aberrant noose

Twosome broadcast—Anti-penis palisades

Perforate sex mashnote capsize stems lizard to crackle with

Commentary tripod lowered panties unisex reel-to-reel

X-ed out tube junk to tie up stiletto convertible floor sips—

Jewel crush blindfold, mineralization unchassising.

For sale /SLASH/ thermostat aping kiss blotch

Lollipop manger Dreamsville diatribe two-way suss—

Whoosh aside—*hex factor.*

Polkadots nylon mousetrap refrain, refrain—[Pills tempi]

Mother popcorn in chains.

Telemarketing your feces.

Pinprick tranquilizing fastness.

Fireworks more luscious to be dissonance.

Sword prell meat mock romance

Buccaneer nylons, black-eyed syrup to

Sharecrop pith-junkies, target rotation

Tropically gangplanked classic aboriginally loco

Tomb of the cow condom cactus marbleize shiny crustracean infidel

Verismo antic skid to pepper insurance with winglike recruitment:

Goggle clemency, a neck adds scream teeth swastika—

Ideologue Advisory

Attitude décolletage

Surgical alert at microbe sell-out—confectionary

Shout-outs on a mass oral crutch—

Frame text ditty pullover missiles.

Dizzy bulb capillary surrender.

Bulk wrench debut Loverhead, pander pause all fuselage—

How much do they charge to talk back?

Every finger in every mouth is group dyslexia.

Bifocals in the foodchain.

[47]

Shuffleboard capsize worker bouquet merengue

Every gang a friend, coupé bunching showboat

Rip down *Award* pin-ups, twin lag gawk

Misunion nipple cake insignia

Teen scale wig applause shame reprising jury method—

Ink frosting bite.

Prop pig decapitates dog.

Pagoda spurts dire ethno-actuary infraction in the spore tilt—

Frontierist skeleton.

One long fadeout

Can It Start Fires?

Beguile wants want curio prefab out our of our outs beleaguer
clotting glisten, it's a coathanger law if you put to try down one
word altogether extra realistic curt learns too people think yep
yep reprogram the [CAPS] mother inattention craves off own
intimacy outside out of the past, the drowsy sloppy fucked look
sporting your calibrated swamp; if only . . . commas its pent on
crime crisp occupancy cauterize a pin lithe over sunset who the
jerks by tentativeness as if big statistic your closet-case close-up
vacuuming disintelligently, well . . . kukla pentad of lamplight
pheromone sensor High Lit mashing a bobbin, large coded inert
to take precedent as expansionism all from regularity around the
campfire's burning better best phantomize the curve the habit
out or hubbed even prone'll do it to gulp give verse for disrespect-
ing cowboys' rope-a-dotage unity misqueue align de-pablummed
daughter to purchase as your rearguard?, or is it hanker coven
strategy as detonation dares you—predicate the want-ad if prod-
ucts could do your mitosis for you circumventing horizon 'as if'
ballot haven frontal praise against all self-rubbing: *bear down* on
the jack zonked for arms precise arms over your sporadicism, or
social score to give it that bad purity translation touch, little
sinny items single up single gumption tips out twice corrupt
bastion of some walkietalkie speech rhythm mal-leveraging any
uni-tab hyphenationist phrase: bracket phooies, boobs transient
as monocled mania-clad anti-incisors & heart's on as its graph
paper foretaste, as its cloud chamber experiments with ambition,
furtive fugitivity seethes covert already cross-violatings in a
base/superstructure huddle for so-called *respect* in access to *brain
bidet* pent up powders awky move awry sensation shun 'ease' to
flatter, gizmo appends calamity by side-show filch hurt time
resharpens—& that's on redirect—by reckoning sideways up to
solipsistic Santa Claus, your tough could be roast declamatory
alien guilt to cede the wide-angling nerves on any of their limbs,
refrigeration abstain soft anorexic vigor immense if innocent

actual is hideous for symptoms—given enough grants, the mice find fault, this perspicacious insect upholstery prozac selfed by tiny noisemakers, some slap initialing a rudiment—do your dreams have tape-hiss, bad resolution?: so fuck your "pedaghoul," contractions that help to circumnavigate, still bubbling drink before kiss call?—in the smear on cell every flash gummed gussied the sec pics pre-op velveteen traditionals [here tip in funny layout] fully published in the hosiery sleep bad before magnetizing that *see it is the get it*—but Sarah, you're a novelist, everything is multi-perspective—party people say CAPS—& own two heads that stature shelf the facts to stand on their own (sold on) (based, biased) FACT—bust not want not.

Please Please Did

please please did ploy goad cursive
putty crush the prompt kinkage curves
objects prevaricate
commotional sibling
martians at a pre-op
afterimaged, bubbly thrall, labial ambush
wake up the objects
as displaced homeowners
catheter fallout—
no just manic—
it's a blotch-up, *the trigger*
wanna wanna
postulates per peep, tongue pending
any gesture is autocratic, jambalaya
formalist frenchkissing
curlicue taking prisoners
I keep in touch in falsetto
the howdy psy-tease gambit
skid me up & miniaturize the jumpstart
terse jamming the acolytic lapdog interval
your name on the afterthought
men gang up on their egos
delirium zoning bouncing sister
fleshhand-me-downs miniaturizing tourniquets
a stereopticon in pink
viewfinder flagrance
a microencumbered shimmygram so
I'm in veto prison
ovals can wait
structure only sudsier, membrane knowhow
& the slogans are backseat driving
vice versa means inventory, drowsier
nudge mammal somersaults

sodajerked the verbs
dummy empire pollen pagination
envy protocol
I do not fear imaginary attack
doped millions up as coma surrogates—
you want international competitiveness, I want
domestic productivity—
let protons be beatniks
civil jelly
assertively torso tilt lilt neck sensate cuddles
muss up your skeleton or memorize the accidents
candy-box adjective butter the end
boast whiplash donor arms
okay is better
heh heh tilt, sit-spin
I want franchising, angular floorshow
searchlights doubt what want
sillier commas—Don't Cross This Out—
I'm a testcase you're a testcase
pattycake yolk swoop & swoon
the cross-taffy tongue billboards pinpoint
crisscrossing phlogiston makeover—
do squids gamble?—
cash nominals neurons unionize
menacing the mutual bloodstream gonzo psychic downtown
stet with an attitude to short out
commune-pink puppy-frosted bearclaw—
so many boys, so little time—
gerund plié gonad cupcake
big stark anaestheticism
blurb out of order or
pulls on the *fatale*
cooler than facts might be

chemistry-correct surprises are fuck-ups
let's overlapse
gimme gimme gimme
global cheerleading hybrid as two-step
cucaracha metonymy
monster wiggle bubbles off
meantime for glowworms stupendously pillowed
froth magnetizes tonya two-fer
nostalgia with a handle—
can we *evolve* now?—hep leash
word honey
crypto-glandular mistletoe with epaulets
lightning's gland, cellularly gooey
or marsupially vertical
senselessness takes care—
we got excited & ripped it off
legs in reverb, so, *I abbreviate*
wait till the applause dies down
on the back of your neck, apprentice posse
cathexis bug-eyed pure corral
headlit as bad partycake validity—
osmosis gets me down
tactile test trash taste skin collage
before the systematizers get jobs
de facto you
metaphor-voyeur
sulphurize curtsified
crayon upstart
getting out the dentist on that thought

Mob

Child Mob: Let those without skin cast the first rip-up. Cells sell unsplit goof sweetheart compression shows off a plusher claustrophobia antidote. All surrender is tone-deaf. Repo post-person law junked crooning neural guarantees as chaste as blood saluting tongue-tied equidistance. Rule fillips. Disbelief in bump form, statues mucked binoc up, blank or perverse, contaminatal *between* crying into zip-lock intoxicated depedestalizing rearview close-ups. Scary caress—"*awake*"—it gets better outside evidence to uncock the facts at the bias infirmary. Frame rouse mass stunts, excise botch, extort exhorts mavericking dollar saps duple lit up adhesive atheist stylus. Even a trifocal wouldn't provide you with this. Sentences ticking, syllable detonators to choke the bully because readers can foam common sense just dispersed as lacandone dwelling. Scatsung subtleties & colossalized jumpstarts, face exit visa curtsy headbang incision rebait. Fondle scares in hyperkinetic insouciance: only the unimaginable is timeless so resistance sets the alarm. (And parenthesis blocks out fake intimation.) Mascara vaccine. Word swoon. Overeat speech. He becomes a deserter only to find Carmen losing interest. Easy pets pink or red underjerked the dual as dust-up, species gets raucous. Blow disjoint honey hybridizes syntax oligopoly. Promissory holes, kick back the covers. Yesplussed rigor mantis heat squad explosion as protocol co-exit frag wacky curvy tends bricolage of circumnugatory burns. Ruse shoulds: "playhead" "jumboized" "INTERPOPS"— the stasis-jeopardy kit pining the shocks. No shun fun, A-line molecules. Reality, that mica. Pry *más* albinoed veins. Seme riotous cenote of indiscretion. The elusive revs up story as loin-words' exemptive trigger better than staccato. The impersonal get better subheads to lure valentines out of breath. Verb squids skull sale. Disruption builds a context convinced as probe retributive rehab booksale—cursive flesh meteorologically abrupt deprotocolloids to step up other flesh postcozying limit tug cling flak system claque. Lips bolt the ballot licking the surplus. Are the prototypes absorbent? I'll lie if I want to. Lick your wounds on your own time. Only open rebellion plaintive. Only the impossible is intimate enough. X Y Z book ends between plural.

Danger Risk Hazard Jeopardy Peril

"Words
were
what
were
whole
what
wasted
words
want
waiting
whose
travel
there"

— Have Having Needful Don't Nothing Needed Can't Don't No Method Vent Another's Aim Fatherless Why Head Inflammable Paradise Known Constituents Quits Existed Sleep Somewhere Hoped for Husband Pit Hypotheses Vanity Depths Dwelling Does Talking Treasure Tales History Dark Inducement Pigment Prongs Offers Nouns Never Noun Eastern Other Remark Another's System Pimps Whooped Doesn't Reference Loopholes Even Erect Hand Material Subject-Matter Me Expedients Impresses Always Masturbation Side Akin Sleepiness Choice Without One One Impends Here Harangue Anxiously Lucky Kindness Size Assault Affairs Face Façade Stuff Face Just Hand Excessively Me Momentum Lustre Even Expeditious Susceptibility Status Flaps Basting Pronouns Rose Recorded Noise Retort Something Frankly Any Regards Sure Presumptuous Sure Couples Boss Verified Verify Doesn't Solves Gossip Abundance However Ghost Choice Signification Surface Lonesome Smoothing Gently Buries Anxiety Obstructed

Task Totality Gate's Suspense During Under Bleed
Details From Governing Contrary Strangers Longing
Lower Must Tricky Sordid Terms Temblor Top Enjoying
Pangs End Totally Have Having Twists Had Threshold
Touch About Dexterity Fitly Envy Suspense Tuned
Friendly Hardly Afflict Impulsiveness Who Words
Without Booking Head Accounts EQUALS Clitoris
Photograph End Idioms Object Ballast Face Concoct
Profusion Diversely Should Peevish Outside Cutting-Edge
Different Delineate Objects Chilly Stress Fluent Physical
Goal Secure Especially Hooked Contingencies Gifts
Obscurity Nozzle Sufficient Short Glaringly Lies
Messenger Constant Notorious Knowing Hampered Interval
Everywhere Statement Quit Eluded In lieu of Roof Device
Darkness Flings Shocks Everything Meant You Many
Dumb News Expedient More Hammer Minutes'
Tomorrow Precautions Pose Thorax Problem Picture
Gradations Notwithstanding Solid Solo Sweetly —
Significance Courage Any Blue Someone Somewhat
Onward Any Anyone Someone Audaciously Someone
Beforehand Breath Enfranchised Partner Properly
Everything Under Awakening Back Expanse Grip Flung
To her To me Flat Glancing Memoir Tomorrow Guise
Nothing Never One Opposite Beside Heed Addicts
Previous Maybe Properly Favor Should Petitions Dialog
Swallowed up Counterfeiting Sleeps Disappeared Dwelling
Behind Dilating Doubt Skill Charmer Enlarged Tumults
Livelihood Avenge Smuggle Spots Foresees Writers
Feasible Scheme *Poesia* Putting Peculiar Nothing System
Unintelligible Another EQUALS Perpetual Poses Display
Salons Super Following Substance Alone If Besides
Succeed Sentenced Drowsiness Site Rumours Ever Feel
Deceits Tranquility Being Nothing Rights Figure–eight

Pronoun Repelling Gown Who Confesses Thumbs Author
Haven Pranced Swerving He Back Events Prior Figure
Whacks Fit Fond Enough Groping Vanity Nativity
Exaggerated O.K. Soaks Admissible Idiots Nebulae Hurt
Onset Partner Helpless Night Say] Verge Service Unwrap
Interval Fancy Somewhere Stars Is What Avenge Is
Vocable Variegated Who Lore Better Motive Thought,
Rosette Decisions Crammed Retrieved Gazing Backbiting
Mental Anything Comrade Enjoyable Anxiously Helpless
Furnished Childish Definite Of it It's Findings Equals-
Sign Stretch Susceptibility Talking Text One Conspicuous
Prompt Queer Regret Words Foresee I Tardy Circumspect
Known Signified Ghosts Fit Simulate Teeters Without
Pinch Unless Smack By Design Divisions Cause Nearing
Motive Tenor Casual Fetuses Whole Divergence Duration
Transverse Account Tightened Possessive Corona Bed
Suspension Small Conscientiousness Compelled Country
Nearing [Danger risk hazard jeopardy peril] Shape Escape
Sight Privy Among Perspective Advances Fit Darling I
Cycle Stroke Verb Quarters Making up Proximate
Whispers Meanwhile Sea Spherical Nouns Published Light
Pose Odd Plentiful Habitat Edges It Distance Head I
Judging I Skin Can't I Civils Irregular Dark Exact
English Vexing Odds Respects Laugh Quick I Words
Blows Delineate Secretive Inference Corpses Convex
Creatures Eloquent Exempt Yo Yo Comrade Cracking
Coveted Meant Occluded Place Latest Curvature Vocable
Glancing Noise Gotten Hoping for Noise Feign Façade
Touching Obscurity Could Would Swarms Solicit
Indefinitely Big Sooner Size Suffering Mania Surrenders
Cacique I Lore Open Mixed Coveted Incident Hoping
Sea Occult Ceiling Abandoned Intimacy Difference
Rumour Uvular Prying Starts Abound Conformable I

Interior Hint Permissions Machine-made Private Deprave Teasing Old-fashioned Matters Even Minus Whisperings Might Length Apportioned Foremost Falling Spacious Conspicuous Endless I Memory Minus sign Bothering Shocks Artifice Hairless Logical Sentenced Deadly Erect Peel Tropes Throat Bulk Fling Space Explanation EQUALS Premises Parry Clamours Farther Kin Pass-words Stable Wooed Author Hitting upon False-hearted Start Facing Inches Like Quick Scheme Ravenous Spectacle Findings Local Mangle Motive Flux Exist Deface Mmmm Bonfire Listen Public Teeny Refuge What Questions Talking Plus Legatos Relation Confirmed Recursive Light.

[This is a translation and rearranging from Spanish of the piece PELIGRO which 'translates,' by rearrangement of word by word materials, an earlier piece JEOPARDY into Spanish]

Valentines

Affection   ———   would be revolution enough
Blitz   ———   dote
But   ———   I thought?
Croon   ———   dazzling
Content   ———   heart's decoy
Croon   ———   croon
Decompose   ———   I could I'm so clumsy
Digit   ———   one emotion per
Empathy   ———   candied
Events   ———   are prodigies to flesh
Fanfare   ———   tripwire
Forever   ———   the moment before the social makes mere titled
everything looks exactly alike
Grip   ———   counterpointed gap
Hand   ———   1. ransoms 2. interchangeable
Head   ———   heart's gauze
Heart   ———   flesh as headrest
If   ———   so
Inflammations   ———   of the present
Inundation   ———   hinge
The Judgmental   ———   burned to the ground
Lacemakers   ———   for Words are Themselves
Lap   ———   beams
Mandatory   ———   Si Si
Milky Way   ———   fool's gold
Momentum   ———   tactile delegation
Mouth   ———   arpeggiation of the given
Near   ———   many-sided
Oomph   ———   by reg
Ornament   ———   truth function
Parataxis   ———   body alive with
Please   ———   1. don't let me be misunderstood
2. crybabied our hearts in the

Precious	———	causality, or else, we're apes
Self	———	graffitification
Sex	———	by parallelogram
Silk	———	to be talk
Sleep	———	the wax without impression
Sunset	———	end-stopped
Tumble	———	cull
Unsaid	———	secretly pronounced
Vary	———	sped up
Veneer	———	can say yes
You	———	we

Reverb Sallies

1.

Time, that condom, a deep beeper

Scoot erasers' persuasive imprecision: it was forehead

slapping enunciative late-comers—curl up asterisk

whose speed-up doorknob phobe yoked at the top to stagger

this rigor. Bubbles are ubiquitous. Socially pulling at

bumbler preview rasp of culpable pout

targeted by skunks

nub of the misfire.

2.

Incognito nutrients encore belies dousing the caterers

luckmore drowsy synergy

flocked adjective cull pix core swarm

maximalistically same as wrung

future tense = catastrophe mid-sentence

nightmarish jitters let the jettisoning begin

convective dough warp safe antidotage—

impulse dwarf clues ripen

tripwire suds. Only habits are fake

captions made of money

3.

Bunk of nonchalance any less half-life

as if death had its subletters. Photosynthesize

me some other way.

Abbreviate the slur, self-induced innocence —

pup-melodic fold-worn teeny index. Proto-

dubs worse than touch indent the glossy

factional inaccessibility, belies sense curly endorphins

oop in print neck

kisses overendebted.

4.

Perspectival sugar declinist

bop on

ocular humid gameplan cyclone stars distort

index slopes gag writhe chute convex tricks.

I'm overorganized. Touring the legible astringency

rondo. Anything precise is too stagey—

havoc per nudge

prostheticizes

length pills up

bends of rhythm. Insert aria

Scale is free.

Fit time with silencer.

5.

Can we gurgle? Smack tumult

suds decoyed incognito cells

inconducive & dizzy traversing transverse

languidity in print. Stave cringe off

smarty ounce lascivious as all get-out—

dispersion of infra-fact give up

clown quack the neck quiver the name's

sucrose debits, pinpoint excess.

Stump the curve

bending the bounce.

6.

Mannikin mystery intimidates

pamper bone buke suddener slur

sass the spite, a density of overlevitation

undulation undulates. Books for testicles, preponderant

napping—dispersively speaking. Caricature capsizes

honorifics on a downward slide

hoop-and-a-half

flatteryless

fontic body droll beleaguered sublimation

makes me want to disown words

dirigibly glued.

7.

I'm not surgery delicacy so

sugar-free the characters become

spray-cans to let the syntax

do the italicizing dosage zoo

extant misnomer—TUMULTER—

getting pretty conglomerate. Labile tumble

dizzy co-dilation off-of, tilted

the flub mesmerizing

iota: divulge the

hoist your

meta-messages are showing.

8

A rumble over gravity cache

niche apt allures

reminiscent iridescent tilt-a-world facade

cuts the delegative *shoulds*, sloganize eyelids

perceptually flagrant sultrier contagion

glossary lets us down. Am we

romance

yet? I mean, can we eat nameplates?

Training is believing.

Tenderness, hackwork

nuzzle up the chunky apropos vibratory furioso.

9.

Can we get to the twizzlers?—

intricate passionately abjured melod

deliriumvirate loan surge, handlit

coquette losses the living bedecked

images racked up festive errata—consequentialism:

serenity comes with aftertuck ready

ready progressivism. Get ovals skit

dead on speck flock can't mezza-reflex

delight as horizon world

taste good impartially accessorized.

10.

The private previous cueup—double red

hammered up the light pictoemphatic

semaphore per person I'm any less capitalized letters

icepickish horizontal

hold zoom sic kino cuss

enswerved—the anti-fuck proscenium over

face *youp* nest into

lit reverse motive splats

the cherry duet—which

emotional sustenance group?

Empathy is guilt.

11.

Megaphonic do the mobile popcorn

fête waltzy second ease skin

pomp friction alloy

desdemonad poco loco

pagination oxygen perpetual sting

pink frosting completely sentenced

gushing artery sense hydra

hoopla to live in the brand names

perf time zoned *olé touché*

hysteria galore cheek headtrip percolate

boomerang

due glassine blow-ups.

12.

Any blur is a grammar. Surety quick supple oust

device flash joker cut up honey

honey purple ur-hope pump & coax lo-leil

auto boy otherwise synapse bed but done

stirred flares the secondists *bon marché*

bundance binge the doppler—

sperm is low cholesterol?—

idlier recourse upswing put-on.

13.

Sideways recoup all-over

bend lilt socially edible aberrant makework

carnally diagrammatic mesmerizing with maracas:

phylum privacy all-over pinpoints greatly cinched

siren florid. Commas treat latent enough for

couples, duststorm of diversion—

hyphens, move over. Interruption

is fallacious ornamentally insisting to

turn nothing upside-down.

14.

Triggers a cuddle caper, spatio-tampering

volumeless agent nudge. INFO.

Assert depth will be all full-

up, it's just, boom: some one plush

raptive vex me a merge eneral guistic

buttering up the teasing any

interval results.

Very up inlaid my head is put on

clerically forms, fonts and logos.

15.

Why is lack always sheer?—*who daunts*

intercom whatsit. Intermittence makes me up.

Transition wets thought through thought

cultivating collusion peeled off the sources

deliver this bunny, hope to vex

any more identical spacing, excisions

wrecked by delicacies bobs to proof beehive

hoplessly fleshy neon—the end of the beguining.

16.

SWEETIME *omni* besideswipe

horizon alarm. Nothing coherent

satisfies. If only hints big pumpkin conspires

could talk louder! Anti-oxidantal *rush*

stems galore compulsion to skittish swoosh

arrears. R.E.M. pulse sparkle

long-distance act promises fact, foggy curl

interstitial throb—decorate

the tumbler delight pretends

the past got ahead of us.

17.

Drowsy favor fancy dazzle fervent

tremors ovally chewier

sleek, outsized. Exit calamity cut up so small

I pinch off the tops, louder beds uphill

whirl aloha pointy-toed anti-tedium—

live free or dust. Fanciful

mardi-gras buds unfamiliar, agitation barely visible

heart loge

measuring distance out in time spoons.

18.

Night empties luck. Gifitishly duty gazing

flambé jolts, happenings overaccosted . Eyeliner

too noisy. Anxious

cell flavor icon index regs.

I need supertitles—silvering voiceprint pout puffs

even slender before adjunct caress insomnia—

busters, lullaby saturated aftershock signing

pencil no-fault.

Heart touches afterbeat

menagerie of

the tenderness reliquary cinderella claimant.

19.

Disshevel this missing you—firefly better brittle

code pleas, puffs, talk about bedspreads poaching liquid

pressure gravitates fruit as lesson book sundown sting

momentum scars dubious plaything subminiatures, go-go

unbent exclamation—this is the putting up of hands.

I'm bleeding dreams

fill up the armslength peter pan air.

20.

Do I really have windows? Used to forgotten

absentmindedly lighthearted 6 mm cultured pearl

tuttifrutti curfew clamor svelte

stir counter-transference nomenclature. Lazily excise

sunset anteed clouds higher, starring you. The virtual

unhinges

room iced sedative scoop is: slapstick X-ray.

Earliest earlier hurry loud indentation lips—

dayglo nerves terrif.

21.

Poly-lapped missing in action. Flares must have

a *vis-à-vis* pent-up page *yet fun—*

waver wander winner jittery

to say so. What rhymes with both?

Your hands go backwards chintzy lingo chocolatier

lavisher seizing

transparency, poifect pajama

outside less heady fluffed

prose chandeliers, solitary colors

22.

Title banquetized. Nestle the. Let's
breathe that. Syllable treason touts born to
smooth put-on neck broth blackened audibly
honeymoon in retrograde. Gilding the. Are we ever
ever? Bright blue. Singed extra I'm overguessing
sedition penitentially humid obliging—qawwali
entire fortune body. Stipulate the crunch soaking
the priorities silence thumps.

23.

Throe's bend

lease the bluff. Interior pilgrimage resuscitated epaulets.

I'm sorry my glasses are steaming up. Objection!

Sustained. Juke in-between indifferently reasonable

faux reverse déjà-vu to soothe via

accelerator. What about? Gloveless

flunk sultrier

crookedness dictate decor chill soars fabulous blossomy

save-all. Two to tango

nonsequitur favorite wet.

24.

Traajectory of enigma resolution

perfunctory distraction dessert. Details of the hammerlock

multiple chemical sensitivity fun & teethe fandango

recluse. Submit! Premature cue, planet of the napes.

Tongue commandeer

midnight primavera tracery echolalic

the heat sweetheart energy twist-off tumbledown

teflon nerves. I say so no.

Only the wings are sweet.

25.

Smooth lectern wah-wah, gaudier fortress

mimetic on command, autobiographically incipient—

a one-legged sky thrills squander, a flammable cuddling

delic' tinsel avidly forgetful. Mail

redishevels foci lovers to look at

your integers. This uncommodified tenderness, token

carousers belie guise hush

to heat the lime, ellipses have everything

love you.

Definition

A

A	——	on how
Abandonment	——	publicity
Abbreviations	——	magnolias
Abrasion	——	profit at bay
Abrupt	——	ripe
Abstraction	——	indifference
Abuttal	——	your skull
Action	——	cuckold
Active	——	neural
Actor	——	avidity
Admixture	——	to the fuzz
Adoration	——	adoption
Adore	——	to pretend
Adultery	——	"a slice off a cut loaf is never missed"
Adventure	——	their plurality against directness
Affidavit	——	potentiometer
After-life	——	up my anus
Ageism	——	documentary
Agnostics	——	to foretaste
Air	——	as nausea's competitor
Akimbo	——	desweatering
Aladdin's lamp	——	shock troops
ALIAS	——	BIGS
Altruism	——	habit's
Am	——	his was the
Ambition	——	1. then near
		2. unproof station
America	——	a Beautician
Anchorage	——	redness of
And	——	to make reasons worse
An Angle	——	supposes

An Animal	——	rule
Antipathy	——	by wonder
Apart	——	swerve
Ape	——	fiction
Aphrodisiac	——	interval
Apparatus	——	self-love
Apparel	——	a night itself
Appeal	——	drink the blood
Appease	——	defaced
Applaud	——	command
The Arbitrary	——	re-outfitted as cotton candy
Arclights	——	on the gerund
Arms	——	as clichés
Art	——	confuse distributive
Aside	——	feminizably
Ass	——	mousse
Astrology	——	viceking
Astronomy	——	for masturbators
Atmosphere	——	gift for commerce
Atmospheres	——	vertical
Atom	——	bullethole
Attention	——	fruit of evocative
Attitude	——	missiles
Attracted to	——	reference to specifics, at least
Authoritarian	——	the present tense itself
Autism	——	gappish
Autokinetic	——	taxes
Autonomize	——	bursting twitch
Autonomy	——	1. any care
		2. promiscuity
Avocational	——	propaganda
Aware	——	prosperity
Awkwardness	——	listens hard

B

Baby	——	abusive as a
Backward	——	as throwweight?
Backwards	——	definition
Bailiff	——	as if by self-infatuation
Bait	——	rehearse
Baiter	——	was to be
Balcony	——	to risk a tree
Ballet	——	error
The Bastard	——	a craze
Beauties	——	syntagm
Bedpan	——	a threat to the end
Beehive	——	keyhole
Beheading	——	an argument
Believability	——	harm
Belladonna	——	piles up as skin
Belong	——	your thwarters
Bereavements	——	cofactions &
Betrayal	——	a triangulation
Biceps	——	those irrationals
Bilingual	——	pauses
The Bind	——	ploy powers
Bingo	——	as dumb as
Birth	——	annuity
Black	——	only that lasts
Bliss	——	okay
Blonde	——	suburb
Blood	——	somersault
Blowhard	——	what the visionary has to say about the skeptical dissociative
Blowtorch	——	ground zero
Blue	——	Procedure

Body	1. never a mirror
	2. a bad loan
	3. garnishee
Bodycount	equal pay
Body image	teachable
Bogus	aped the
Bomb	everyone is a dummy for a bigger one
Bone	no
Bonus	leaps
Boop boopie	boop boopie parenthesis repeat parenthesis
Bootzilla here	pull my string
Boys	are cordials too
Brave	liquid
Breach	reparries
Bright	warns
The Brittle	is what speeds
Brutus	fold the napkins
Bubble-eyed	Day One
Bubbling	gossip
Bulkish	uneddying
Business	to be signs again
Butane	from behind
Buzzarding	financial
By the hour	no nouns

C

Caesura	——	DECOY
Cake	——	1. cake till later
		2. suffocates
Cakewalk	——	1. hysterectomy
		2. toolbox
The Candy	——	out of uniform
Cannibal	——	insult
Capture	——	to make fun of
Career	——	autism
Careful	——	total
Catalogs	——	your eyes
Categories	——	self-debauching
Catharsis	——	drone
Ceiling	——	hope chest
Center	——	putrid
Chafed	——	switched waist
Chainsaw	——	*whose* chainsaw
Chamber of Commerce	——	religion
Chance	——	a sabotage
Chandeliers	——	our heaven
Chastity	——	1. a headless line
		2. paraplegic enough
Chewy	——	decipherage
Chiasma	——	to you too
Chill	——	oscillation
Choke	——	nearness us
Christlike	——	condoms
Circuit	——	lesson
Citizens	——	anti-cavity
Civic	——	money
The Clearing	——	a concentration camp

Climaxes	———	obfuscatory
Closet	———	op. cit.
Closure	———	genre
Coldness	———	art colony
Coercive	———	in response to
The Collapse	———	embroidered
Color	———	leisure
Coma	———	career
Comeback	———	evidence recombinant eclipse
To Commit	———	always assessing
Comparison	———	bad retort
Complication	———	had preceded it
Concentration	———	only psoriasis
Con	———	wobbled by slam
Concoct	———	disaster
Conductivity	———	conferred offspring
Confession	———	a bit Euro-trash
Conformist	———	money
Congealed	———	thrall
Conniption	———	non-image
Connubials	———	buttered up
Conquistadors	———	localized
Consciousness	———	anal
Consider	———	Error
Constative	———	yolk his state
Contents	———	slivered!
Continuity	———	abusive
Contort	———	*yet yes*
Contrast	———	a myth
The Converse of every statement	———	childhood
Copula	———	off-wax
Copyright	———	by torsos
Cornice	———	zorro

Credibility	———	headlining
Credit	———	rhubarb
Creed	———	fond
Criss-crossing	———	uninfatuated
Cronies	———	ballpeened
Crush	———	1. enthrive
		2. that blindness
Crystal	———	catheter
Cuddle	———	laminated
Cue	———	severance
Curbing	———	the curbing
Currency	———	chance
Curtsy	———	spreadeagled
Curtsying	———	in ticket form
Cut	———	the dunce

D

Dark	——	1. confirms perspective
		2. forgives
/ — /	——	*/ — — /*
Daylight	——	cadging
The Dead	——	not exclusive
Dears	——	blur
Debentures	——	please close eyes
Debt	——	lap
Decisional	——	chameleon
Decisions	——	divisions
Decode	——	that happens one night
Decontextualized	——	inconsistencies
Decor	——	penetration blues
Deer	——	ghetto identical
Definition	——	1. thievery
		2. down for a slow count
Delay	——	could be willing
Denerved	——	throne
Denial	——	yet yolk
Density	——	figure / divide
Deposit	——	innermost night
Deride	——	bent
Derogation	——	to be matriculate with
Description	——	what remorses the object
Desire	——	1. too awareness-prone
		2. power, taught
Desk	——	lambs
Despise	——	conclusions
Destiny	——	image
Desyllableized	——	mirrors

Details ———	1. threat
	2. polyps
Dew ———	impertinence
Dialogue ———	coercion
Difference ———	1. power bends
	2. money says
Dignity ———	a form of greed
Dilate ———	copied
Dioxins ———	totalled
Direct ———	beyond ideology
Discolored ———	example
Discourse ———	self-displaced
Disgrace ———	sum
Dismount ———	single finger
Disputing ———	reducing
Dissent ———	overfingering
Dissuade ———	hover
Division ———	deoxidized
Doom ———	a bash
The Dot ———	1. nothing
	2. wreathed
Dotted eighths ———	locksmiths
Dovetail ———	permission
Dread ———	by footnote
Dream ———	please
Dreams ———	to saturate
Drift ———	kill
Drug references ———	bad teeth of the poem
Drugs ———	grudges
Drumming ———	by cracks
Duel ———	farm
The Dumb ———	a text

Dusk ———— 1. translates the face

2. bugs

Duty ———— 1. *bon*fire

2. getup

E

Earth	——	hope's subsidiary
Economy	——	pre-rubbed
Ecstasy	——	non-transferable
Edgelines	——	paranoia
Effigies	——	it's a one piece
Effortless	——	dire
Eggheads	——	only a quarter to play
Eggs	——	tutorially endentured
Electrification	——	autism
Electromagnetic	——	nakedness
Electrons	——	lonesome
Embouchures	——	no giblets
Emotions	——	purely dyslexic social constructions
Emphasis	——	nonsense
Enabling	——	Surrender
Encephalic	——	party
Enough	——	1. I'm anatomical
		2. one society is
Ensnaring	——	information
Entourage	——	editing
Entry	——	Ornament
Equivalence	——	the trivia is relapsing into
Eraser	——	tautened
Ethnography	——	sibilant enough
Euphemisms	——	the forgiving
Eurhythmic	——	mistletoe
Eve	—	of or own
Everyone	——	in its way
Everything	——	1. your desire
		2. begins in recomposition
Evidentially	——	period

Exaggerate	————	themseltzer
Examination	————	blameless
Excess	————	atoned delight
Exculpation	————	greeting
Excuses	————	hyena
Exempt	————	strut
Ex-husbands	————	random swastika
Expectations	————	1. puce
		2. punctuation
Experience	————	not a misprint
Experimentation	————	the fat language
Extant	————	same
Extreme commonwealth	————	tunnels attached
Eyeballs	————	pretty material

F

[F] ——— act
Facade ——— spore
Facets ——— vices
Facts ——— mandated in the shape of laundromats
Factual ——— font fact front
Fake ——— to exonerate
To Falter ——— the terms
Fat ——— always like this
A Fault ——— 1. pops
    2. indirected
Fear ——— breeds paper
Feeling ——— not fact
Feline ——— disasterish
Ffor ——— if I
Fiend ——— mind
The Figural ——— cash
Finely woven ——— Third World
Finesse ——— crawl into
First aid ——— attitude
Flaw ——— crease
Flesh ——— 1. collective
    2. far more decisive
Flesh tone ——— small events
Flower ——— comes to order
Fluid ——— total fumble
Fluke ——— acceleration
Flute ——— peeps buyer
Focal ——— investing
Fog ——— as euphoria
Foolings ——— swallow
Fops ——— of my rights

Force	——	to whine
Foreground	——	lack of confidence
Foreign policy	——	a bulimia of
Forever	——	an alternative
Forgiveness	——	a category
Form	——	fame
Formalism	——	is *short*
Fossil news	——	arteries
The Frame	——	exasperated
Framing	——	after-glow
Franchise	——	to be deterred
Freedom	——	1. only makes wanting / more become you
		2. oversight
Frets	——	as alive scale
Frills	——	fondleable
Frilly	——	kinda
Fructifying	——	nameplates
Fun	——	1. naked
		2. loan
		3. sentient
Furtive	——	fool

G

Gad —————— to a stylus
Ganging —————— theses
Gap —————— perhaps
Gaps —————— 1. the welcome mats
2. fake you fade
Gauzy —————— midget
Geisha —————— shortwave or FM
Gender —————— a host
Gender stereotype —————— foreign policy alone
Genital —————— acolytes? accolades?
Genitals —————— so
Gentle —————— vulcanize
Gesture —————— FOR SALE
Gingerbread —————— you *make?*
Gist —————— say curve
Globe —————— this lethal
Gloss —————— busting
Glue —————— executioner
God —————— damp!
Godzilla —————— with help
Gold —————— spelling
The Gooey —————— used to be specific
Gore —————— heraldry
Gown —————— useful ideology
Gram —————— pupil
Grammar —————— 1. tidies up vocational heart-busying glamor
2. toxins
Gravity —————— claustrophobic rhythm or silly poise
Grief —————— Temporal Extension
Grime —————— of co-management
Grotesque —————— privacy

Guilt	————	1. a christening
		2. speed
Guise	————	bugged
Gun	————	throat, literally swollen

H

Ha ha ha	———	sugar
Halo	———	1. hard-on
		2. Mazes
Hard	———	soaking
Harm	———	Matter
Haughty	———	afterthoughts
Havoc	———	the fend
He	———	ugly word
Head	———	black
Headaches	———	gaps beating time
Headshrunk	———	garage
Hearing	———	as writing
Heil	———	putative raw
Hell	———	vacuum
Help	———	1. *Me, Rhonda*
		2. authority
Helter-skelter	———	social
Hems	———	readability
Hep	———	ensconced
Hepped	———	the epitaphs
Hey	———	hey!
Hierarchy	———	genotype
Hips	———	a fiend
To Hit	———	philosophy
Hoax	———	rerun
Home	———	1. as mixer
		2. by eyeballs
Honest	———	to video
Honey	———	1. proof
		2. pillow to our

Horizon ——— 1. its own blur
2. Mask
3. yoke
4. entire uh-oh of interruption
Hostess ——— juvenilia
Hours ——— how many billable?
Hovercraft ——— at risk
Hurry ——— antennae of
Hush ——— arm
Hyacintha ——— gotta dance
Hype ——— the whites
Hyphen ——— prurience
The Hyphens ——— conquered all
Hysterectomy ——— history next to me

I

I ———	1. go open
	2. helm erosion
I agree ———	to be believed
Iced ———	paginated
Ideality ———	repent sequence
Identify ———	as figuring
Ideologic ———	lashes
Idiots ———	decoy gifts
If ———	split when
Ill wind ———	coercion
I'm ———	1. if you
	2. occurs
	3. destined to be Product Evaluation Consultant
Image ———	1. clinic
	2. destiny
Imagized ———	the doting
The Immediate ———	is Conjunction
Impalpable ———	leans
Impatience ———	inner
Impediment ———	tonic
Imperial ———	suture
Impersonal ———	imperative
Incentive ———	adjectives
Inch ———	pessimistic traction
Inclusives ———	reinvested in
Incoherence ———	nonresistant
Indented ———	smotherers are
Indicative ———	clutter
The Indistinct ———	bedding
Ingestion ———	diorama

Ink ———	1. surrender flag
	2. 'made the paper'
Innate ———	room under synapse clips
Innocence ———	amoeba'd
Inordinate ———	literature
Insignia ———	bovine
Insults ———	destylizing
The Insuperable ———	open to temptation
Intent ———	hound of
Intentio ———	stubborn prejudice
Interact ———	is a fuck up
Interest ———	empties
Interested ———	you're?
Interim ———	treatings
Interims ———	hyperbole
Interior ———	pretty distanceful
Interval ———	would be too fertile
Intervals ———	we have your best ones at heart
Intermarriage ———	leisure
Intimacy ———	strike-prone
Intravenous ———	napalm
Intrusiveness ———	too narrative
I.O.U.s ———	backlit
Irony ———	1. wiretaps
	2. Discipline
Is ———	You
Isinglass ———	dearer
Isolation ———	my understudy
I won't ———	too

J

Japan	——	"gales of creative destruction"
Jargon	——	the imputed
Jelly	——	safety first's
Jet	——	so loose
Journalism	——	flavor intimidation
Journalists	——	mere betters
Judgmentally	——	whited
Jurisdiction	——	spirochetes
Jury	——	spasms
Just	——	sign your last name
Juxtaposition	——	juice

K

Keystoning ———— infidelity
Kid ———— foreclosure
Kin ———— iris
Kindness ———— as artisanal
Kissing ———— set-up reversions
Kith ———— vains
Kitsch ———— to go
Kitschy ———— glue
Kudos ———— miniaturize?

L

Lack of quality	——	lack of courage
Laments	——	retinal
Language	——	an abstract of its own fluidity?
Larvae	——	1. discourse
		2. gimmicks like pearls
Latitude	——	no no no no
Laughs	——	when it zips backwards
Lavalier	——	putsch
Law	——	wants its dangle into the picture
Leather	——	soliciting
Left	——	it *Left* and *Happen*
Length	——	1. a fad
		2. substitutes for talk
		3. culture
Lens	——	forehead
Lesser	——	it noun that
Lesson	——	killed by
Let's	——	retilt
Level	——	lull worms
Lexically	——	acting out
Lick	——	vaya!
Lie	——	court
Lies	——	as snakes
Life	——	sponge it
Limits	——	1. mount the
		2. a trellis over flattening
Limp	——	known
Listening	——	irruptions of hegemony
Literacy	——	folds back
Literature	——	muscle itself
Loans	——	loves pledge

Loop	———	to be together
Loose change	———	ferocious
Loss	———	wrong word
Love	———	interrupting
Loyalty	———	fears the peep
Luck	———	dark
Lump	———	quoted

M

M-16	——	sleeps in my hand
Magnetic	——	duality
Mammal	——	motive
Mana	——	1. cud
		2. nut-hard
Marriage	——	the yellow brick road
Manic	——	providence
Manners	——	the lab course
Maples	——	such druids
Margins	——	aplomb
Market	——	sortie
Martyr	——	to market
Mass	——	Not
Masturbatory	——	punctual community
May	——	maybe
Me	——	1. exaggerate
		2. to-to-to-to
Meaning	——	face of the future
Meanings	——	banditos themselves
Meat	——	soon innocence
Mellowness	——	braindead
Melodic	——	proboscis
Membranes	——	bleachers
Memory	——	current ruling
Mentality	——	sponsorship
Merchant	——	how quaint
Mere dreams	——	ideals
Merges	——	heading
Messiah	——	just skin welt
Metric	——	rhetoric, with fine tuning
Millionario	——	*ven, ven, ven*

Mind ———   1. pine for
        2. below the black
Mirage ———   the symbol of sound progress
Mirror ———   partisanship
Mirrors ———   epaulets
Misbehavior ———   delicacy
Mishap ———   to join
Misspelling ———   likeness
Misuse ———   alike
The Moment ———   in an extension cord
Montage ———   jury
Moon ———   hoax
Morals ———   ethics
Morbid ———   a
Morphic ———   sugarplum
Morphine ———   as pure indication
Mote ———   other
Moth ———   sullied surrogate
Motive ———   cause to reverse
Motto ———   lisp
Mouth ———   1. hood in
        2. to hermit
Multiplicity ———   wholesale
Mummification ———   by refusal of purchase
Muscatel ———   winterizing
Musculature ———   this convivial
Music ———   sociology
Mutant ———   singe up
Mutes ———   spent

N

Name	———	1. hot-sensed
		2. getaway
Names	———	1. wares
		2. trained on the victims
Nape	———	peers
Narrate	———	donations
Narrative	———	surface twin
Nausea	———	your back-up group
The Necessity	———	undresses
Neck	———	1. only effect
		2. interpersonal
		3. breeds delight suggestively
Negation	———	care
Negative space	———	photojournalism
Nemesisity	———	fatal corsage
The Neuter	———	thickens
Night	———	a carburetoration
Noise	———	all court
Normality	———	nerve-gases of
New Years	———	thorazine
No	———	1. America's since
		2. hahahahahahah
The Nobler	———	the affidavit
Nostalgia	———	perjured
Not	———	that you could stop
Nothing	———	but obeys
Nouns	———	1. you go by
		2. see Verbs
Novelistic	———	as ghoul
Novice	———	rubbed in by name
Number	———	sure

O

Oblong	——	endearment
Oedipal	——	scissors
Offensives	——	asterisk
Only	——	roar
Open	——	inattentive
Opera	——	edit out
Opposites	——	maybe go slow
Oppositions	——	making a butter of
Oppression	——	where one moment isn't just as good as another
Opt	——	bauble
Optical	——	on good manners
Oration	——	fold kisses in
Order	——	penny
Organs	——	fiercer
Organza	——	bye
Out	——	banked misdemeanor
Outside	——	Overhearing
Over	——	*voilà*
Overachiever	——	neocolonialism
Oxidous	——	wetting
Own	——	sic

P

Pal   ———   1. by instillments
                     2. lap
Palimpsest ——— combinatorial
Pangs ——— such a resort
Panic ——— ratio
Paper ——— will make you free
Parapet ——— pronoun under
Parenting ——— blot
Parents ——— the thread you deny
Particularity ——— alarms
Parts ——— bits in a storm
Parsimony ——— is for dwarves
Partition ——— the general good
Passion ——— ratio
Past ——— test
Pedagogues ——— paraplegics
Peers ——— forecourt
Penpersonship ——— freezer of
Perestroika ——— malling
Periphery ——— of excitation
Permanent ——— means *soaks through*
Personal experience ——— obediently derivative
Perversions ——— hooks
Philosophy ——— 1. notwithstanding
                     2. is hungry
Phraseological ——— watering
Pillow ——— exempt
Pinnacle ——— turned inside out
Pinwheel ——— juries
Pissing ——— are all dead
Plans ——— a pitchfork to your

Pleasure	———	measure
Pleasures	———	all sequels
Pleats	———	as sitters
Plot	———	cut in proverb
Ploys	———	only
Plumage	———	1. caesuras
		2. daybreak
Plural	———	halo mazes
Plurals	———	futures, markets
Poise	———	1. unkempt in charisma to better purpose
		2. blinks
Poker	———	Dad (house music remix)
Police	———	the only growth industry
Political	———	as hover
Politics	———	testy
Popping	———	origamied
P.O.W.	———	squeezebox
Practical	———	practicable
Presences	———	n'existent pas
Precision	———	dotage
Predecessors	———	now more prosaic
Preen	———	atoll
Preferences	———	abuse
Prejudice	———	more than a little chair
Prepares	———	bogus
Pressure	———	homesickness
Prim	———	pictorial
Prime	———	cakes over
Primer	———	lips
Prior	———	ruckus
Privacy	———	guesswork
Private	———	a little further on
Privilege	———	less neat

Program	———	sap in the peel
Projects	———	mislead backwards
Problem	———	licks the creep
Prose	———	in corsets
Protocol	———	breath by proxy
Provocation	———	qualifies too
Proximal	———	derogatory
Pubic	———	oven
Punctuation	———	would just be precious
Punctuations	———	whatever fellates the intangible
Pure	———	thrust decor
Purity	———	a receptacle
Purse	———	perspective
Pus	———	ontology
Putsch	———	on the quick

Q

Quality ——— overturned machines
Quiet ——— Smear

R

Radio	——	gnawed
Rainforest	——	cover-letter
Rank	——	grasp
Ratio	——	species
Rave-ups	——	can as easily petrify
Reading	——	1. beyond lineage
		2. Rental
Reason	——	remarkably conciliatory
Reasons	——	typographical
Rebetrothe	——	rectangles
RED	——	*itors*
Reference	——	1. so fugitive
		2. valueless without an invoice
Regs	——	in murk
Relationship	——	social chicken
Remind	——	unequals
Renewal	——	dissociative
Repeat	——	repeat!
Resistance	——	warmed by blur
Result	——	sentiment
Retina	——	udder
Retinal	——	quisling
Revenge	——	would be on cable
Reversal	——	custody
Revolution	——	a leisure
Reward	——	ooze
Ridicule	——	constatives
Rights	——	promptbook on my
Risk	——	1. a fucking serious
		2. don't bite
		3. commotions of

Root ———— exultant at raking purity of
Rumor ———— abbreviation enough
Rub ———— from apes

S

Sado-maso	——	salary
Safety	——	gratuity
SAKE	——	aggressively capitalized
Saliva	——	esoterica
Saltpeter	——	doggerel
To Salve	——	adjourn
A Sandbagging	——	as literate
Sanity	——	playback
Sap	——	declension
Sapiens	——	artillery
Sassy	——	pre-op
To Save	——	Punk
Scarbrains	——	your prescriptions are just so many
SCATTER	——	TRADE-OFF
Screaming	——	groups
Scythes	——	lips
Sedimented	——	payback
Seduction	——	dirt
Seismic	——	to the gleam
Seizing	——	to forgive
Self-discovery	——	fit of absent-mindedness
Self-reflexive	——	impotent enough
Self-sustain	——	white lines
Semen	——	tautology
Semiotic	——	Fata Morgana
Sentence	——	a tradition each successive word amends
Sentiment	——	1. monopoly sector
		2. has its mathematicians
		3. counterfeited moebius
Septic	——	secular
Shadows	——	on condom

Shape Brain	——	Alike Lilt
Shatter	——	the hyperactive
She	——	End
Shelf	——	how big are you on my
Shit	——	in operation
Shook	——	as palimony
Sibling	——	premise at random
Sieged	——	baton
Sigh	——	a determinism
Sighs	——	the spatula language
Sightlines	——	syntax
The Signal	——	hung separately
Signature	——	rape
Silence	——	control
Silkworm	——	occluded
Simplicity	——	parabola
Simultaneous	——	your idea of transition
Sin	——	narrative
The Sincere	——	laminates
Single-ply	——	queer
Single	——	decorative exact
Singular	——	you're slunk down in the
Skew	——	you!
Sky	——	tiny filthy
A Slab	——	commotion
Sleek	——	confess this
Slender	——	jack-rabbity
Slump	——	modelling
Slur	——	blue
Sluts	——	sudden
Smile	——	done whitenesses
Smirk	——	with its own organism
Snares	——	you get to keep

Snow	——	however
Snowing	——	I gave it
Sob	——	compliments
Sober	——	fatter
The Social	——	1. garrulity of chance
		2. artificial for you
Social dream	——	unsuspecting
Sociology	——	music
Somatic	——	halo
A Somewhat	——	a someone
Soon	——	poodle until
Sound	——	1. forged
		2. prevents thumbs
Sortilege	——	?
Spatial	——	1. clumsy ellipsis
		2. organs
Specifics	——	the flaws vibrate with
Speech	——	1. putative yearning
		2. as dex
Speed	——	1. proximity
		2. sexed
Spherical	——	not tonight
The Spillage	——	by assigning
Splintering	——	pragmatism
Spurious	——	blood
Sputters	——	parfait
Star	——	swaddling
Starlit	——	nerve abuse
Stasis	——	gift
Static	——	1. bites
		2. war-zone
Stencils	——	skunked
Stills	——	lulls a little

Sting ———— elision
Stops ———— the stopping never
Stripe ———— loss
Structure ———— its Tour-Guide
A Structure Learned ———— a birdcage horizon
Students ———— buy bond
Stumps ———— suck!
Stun ———— exegetical
Stupidity ———— 1. not transgressive
2. a transcript of it
Subliminal ———— blossom
Submarines ———— management
The Suction ———— a promotion
Suddenness ———— bliss
Suffocate ———— chides
Sugar ———— Inscrutable
Sugared ———— Oval
Sultry ———— falsification
Surrealism ———— Overbuilt
Surreptitious ———— collective
Svobodu ———— Freedom!
Syllables ———— electrification
Symmetry ———— tickets
System ———— indelicate

T

Tabula rasa	——	prorate
Tacit	——	glowworms
Tagsales	——	fan out!
Tank	——	diaries
Tango	——	cloture
Tattoo	——	amnesia
Tautology	——	owl feels
Taxing	——	boom
Tears	——	salute
Tedium	——	as a promissory space
Teeth	——	1. vote hole
		2. pravda
Tempt	——	esteem
Tender	——	obstructively
Tenderness	——	arrowed
Tenpins	——	connubial
Testicle	——	the day
Testified	——	hem
Theism	——	shimmy beyond
Thematic	——	clerks
Themselves	——	cohesions of
Theology	——	butter or margarine
Theories	——	an inking
There	——	a world outside
Thicker	——	quicker
Thighs	——	1. you can invent
		2. voiceover
Thinking	——	losing scale
This	——	do not peeve for it
Throating	——	reindeer
Tickled out	——	to ramify

Tinsel	——	my rubies
Tissue	——	too pat
The Title	——	a previous neck
Tone	——	betweenness
Tongue	——	platform
Tongueless	——	tidy
Toting	——	mirror
Top	——	stop
Torture	——	clearsightedness by saliva
Totter	——	earned strife
Touching	——	lessonplans
Traces	——	adjourn
Traditions	——	not worth surprising
Train	——	Entice
Tropicalize	——	lower
Truth	——	1. that's-ocrat
		2. septic
Tryst	——	this exultant
Tuning	——	1. knees tuning
		2. fuck
TWO	——	OF THE SME
Twos	——	feel also

U

Unbuttoning	——	*bonita*
Uncaptioned	——	schist
Unconscious	——	dirt
Uncut	——	I stoop to
Unfaithful	——	grave-robbers of the present tense
Unison	——	soaking; sieve
Unit	——	stet
Up and down	——	theatrical
UPSTAIRS	——	EVENTUALLY
Use	——	1. as fruit
		2. sound excuses
Usherette	——	faction
Usurpation	——	pissout

V

Vain	———	1. you suck in
		2. of another lure
Valid	———	valid valid
Value	———	stockings spelled backward
Variety	———	the sill of secrets
Veins	———	1. night
		2. lemons
Verbs	———	1. attenuations of action
		2. on Deep Background
Virgin	———	valves
Virginity	———	sauvignon
The Virgin Mary	———	that's Linda Darnell, unbilled
Virtue	———	consolation
Void	———	cooed on the void of

W

Waist	——	unallowed
Waltz	——	pneumatism
Wand	——	lather out
War	——	penis so late
Warns	——	talk
Wealth	——	astride
Weekends	——	confiscation
Wet	——	1. users
		2. what sympathy
Whereabouts	——	biology lodestar
Whispering	——	hilt
White-coated	——	pillage
White distance	——	a hand which pivots
Who	——	talents
Whoa	——	wine gone
Whole	——	1. debris
		2. blame
		3. damaged to be in one
Whore	——	from figment to
Why	——	1. dedicated to who
		2. heavier
Wide	——	yellow
Wisdom	——	evasion for ghouls
Wording	——	dissenting
Words	——	phony substitutes for concrete sensuality
The World	——	too late with us
Wounds	——	eccentricities
Wrench	——	bed besides
Wrist	——	boomerangs as coinage
Writ large	——	still breed?

X

X ——— captive

Y

Yoke ——— likes doings

Yolk ——— the hammer

You ——— 1. the tend thing

2. wish otherwise

You need ——— more abstraction?

You're in that mood ——— you must get out of it

Z

Zeal ———— 1. alphabet
2. could covary
Zero ———— prior
Zippers ———— 1. in retrospect
2. heroes to themself
Zoo ———— yes.